FLASHES
AND
BANGS

Simon Mugford

Illustrated by Thomas Morahan

Abrams
Learning Trends

Flashes and Bangs
ISBN: 978-076-645183-4

This edition copyright © 2017 Abrams & Company Publishers, Inc., Austin, TX.

Distributed by Abrams Learning Trends, Austin, TX.
www.AbramsLearningTrends.com

First published in the UK in 2016. This edition is published by arrangement with Oxford University Press.

Acknowledgments

Series Editor: Greg Foot

Inside illustrations by Thomas Morahan

The publisher would like to thank the following for the permission to reproduce photographs: **Cover:** sam72/Shutterstock; **p8t:** OUP; **p8cl:** EcoPrint/Shutterstock; **p8cr:** Ksenia Raykova/Shutterstock; **p8b:** Flip Nicklin/Minden Pictures/Corbis; **p9t:** Scubazoo/SuperStock/Corbis; **p9c:** Phillip Ellard/Shutterstock; **p9b:** Imagefolio; **p13:** MBI/Alamy; **p14:** Seb Oliver; Getty Images; **p15t:** iStock; **p15b:** Jacqueline Veissid/Getty Images; **p16l:** Hulton-Deutsch Collection/Corbis; **p16r:** Bettmann/Corbis; **p17:** Roman Sigaev/Alamy; **p18:** newcorner/Shutterstock; Picsfive/Shutterstock; Galló Gusztáv/Alamy; **p19:** s_oleg/Shutterstock; Arthit Kaeoratanapattama/Shutterstock; OUP; Zoliky/iStock; **p19r:** Jens Buettner/Corbis; **p20t:** Lebrecht Music & Arts/Corbis; **p20b:** Klawitter Productions/Corbis; **p21:** Daily Herald Archive/National Media Museum/Science & Society Picture Library; **p22:** Flynt/Dreamstime; **p23:** Ensuper/Shutterstock; **p25:** Conspectus/Alamy; **p26:** Giles Moberly/Alamy; **p27:** Igor Zh./Shutterstock; **p28:** jun@sa/Getty Images; **p29t:** Larry Mulvehill/Corbis; **p29b:** Fotograferen.net/Alamy

Printed in China   10 9 8 7 6 5 4 3 2 1   OUP/1116/10312

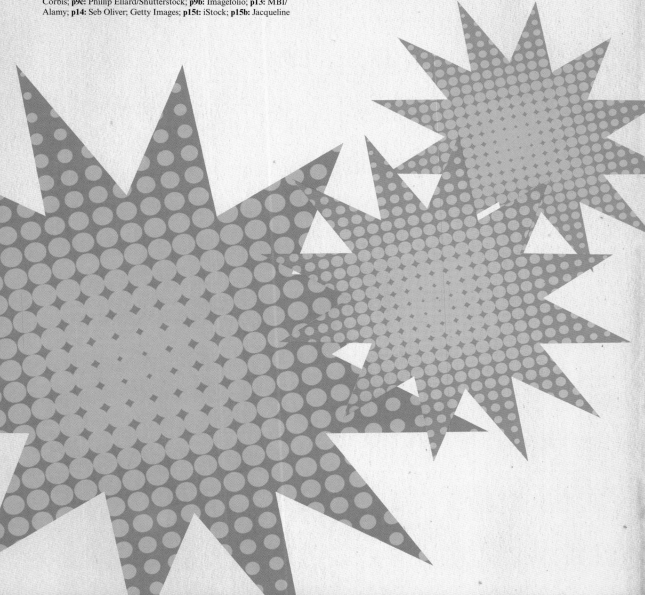

Contents

Bang

What's the loudest noise you can make?

POW!

CRASH!

BAM!

BOOM!

Wow!

That was loud enough to scare your neighbors. Just tell them we're doing important scientific research!

In this book you'll find out all about sounds, however they are made!

Flash

What's the brightest light you've ever seen? (Remember, don't look directly at a bright light – it can damage your eyes.)

We'll uncover the brightest lights and discover what lights up our world.

So, where do we start? Well, let's find out what sound and light are. After that the choice is yours. Page through and if you see something you like, dive right in. It's an A to Z of light and sound!

What is sound?

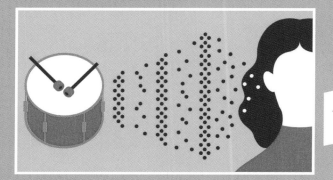

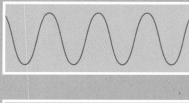

Sounds are vibrations that travel through the air.

A sound starts when something makes the air jiggle around, like when somebody beats a drum. The vibrating drum wiggles the air next to it, which bumps into the air next to that. These wiggling **vibrations** carry on all the way through the air to your ear.

We often draw that vibration as a sound wave like this:

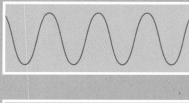

Some sounds have lots of vibrations bunched close together. These are high-**frequency** sounds, like a referee's whistle at a football match.

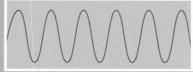

Some sounds have fewer vibrations. They are low frequency – the lower the sound, the lower its frequency. Just like a big bass drum.

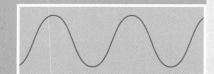

What is light?

Did you know light is a kind of wave too? Light works a bit like the Wave. In the Wave people's bodies go up and down and the wave travels sideways. It's the same for a light wave, but rather than a wave of people, it's a wave formed as **energy** vibrates back and forth.

Each color of the rainbow has a different-size wave.

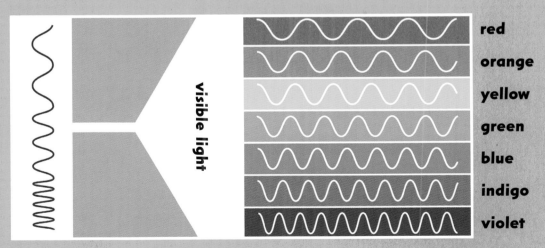

visible light

red
orange
yellow
green
blue
indigo
violet

Red has longer waves so we say it has a longer **wavelength**. Blue has shorter waves and a shorter wavelength.

Amazing animals

There are lots of sounds in the world that we cannot hear. We can only pick up sounds within our **human hearing range**. Low-**frequency** sound below our hearing range is called **infrasound**. High-frequency sound above our hearing range is called **ultrasound**. But guess what? We might not be able to hear these sounds but some animals *can*.

Bats, dogs, and dolphins can hear ultrasound.

Elephants, blue whales, and birds can hear infrasound.

Bright beasts

Not all light is made by turning on a light bulb. In the deepest oceans, strange creatures glow in the gloom. They carry chemicals in their bodies that enable them to create their own light. It's called **bioluminescence** (*say* bigh-oa-loo-min-es-ense).

This Anglerfish has its own lantern that goes everywhere with it. It uses it to attract its lunch. **Gulp!**

Clever chlorophyll

Plants need light to live. A green chemical in their leaves called chlorophyll (*say* clor-uh-fill) allows plants to absorb sunlight, which gives them energy.

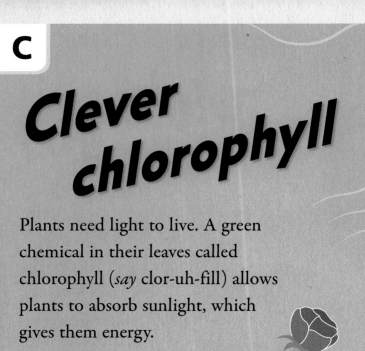

sunlight

oxygen

oxygen

carbon dioxide

carbon dioxide

water

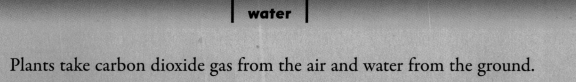

Plants take carbon dioxide gas from the air and water from the ground. Chlorophyll helps plants make these ingredients into two important things:

- food that they use to grow
- oxygen that we need to breathe.

This amazing process is called photosynthesis (*say* foa-toa-sin-thuh-sis).

D

Dangerous decibels

Loud music and sounds can be fun, but too much of these can be harmful! Very loud sounds are made by **vibrations** that have lots of **energy**. These vibrations can damage our sensitive ears.

Loudness is measured in decibels (dB) (*say* de-si-bells). Listening to a sound louder than 85 decibels for more than eight hours can damage hearing. Loudness is also known as **amplitude** – how big a sound wave is.

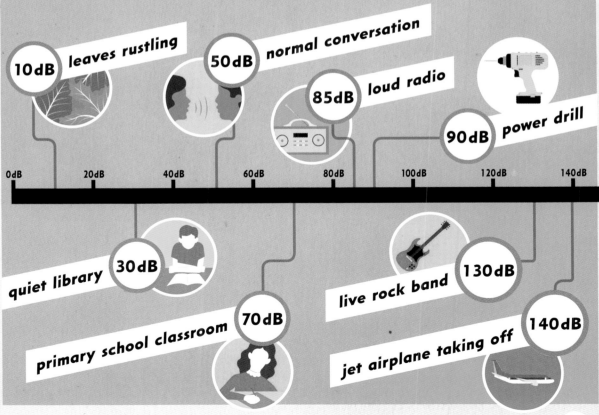

10dB leaves rustling

50dB normal conversation

85dB loud radio

90dB power drill

0dB 20dB 40dB 60dB 80dB 100dB 120dB 140dB

quiet library 30dB

live rock band 130dB

primary school classroom 70dB

jet airplane taking off 140dB

Ears – inside and out

E

There is more to your ear than the part stuck to the side of your head. **1.** The outer ear directs sound **vibrations** into the auditory canal. **2.** The vibrations float along this canal and set your eardrum vibrating too. **3.** This wiggles some tiny bones behind the eardrum. **4.** They set the hairs in your cochlea shaking. **5.** Your auditory nerve turns the moving hairs into a message that it sends to the brain. That's how you hear what you hear!

Eyes open

E

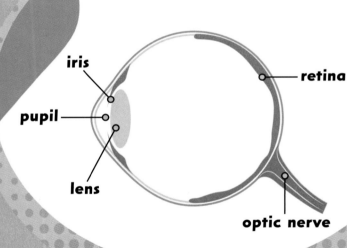

Have you ever thought about how your eyes work? We see things when light bounces off them into our eyes. The light passes in through a little circle in the middle of each eye called the pupil. The iris stretches and shrinks the pupil to let in more or less light. The light falls on your retina and the optic nerve sends a signal to your brain.

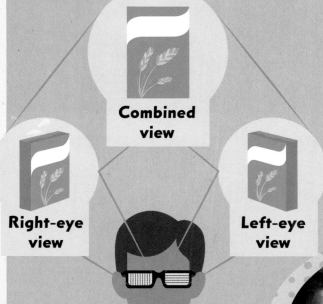

auditory nerve

eardrum

3

5

1

2

4

auditory canal

cochlea

outer ear

Combined view

Right-eye view

Left-eye view

Film tricks

Each eye looks at an object from a slightly different angle, and your brain joins the images together. This is called stereoscopic vision.

A three-dimensional (3D) film is recorded from two different angles and both views are projected onto the screen at the same time. 3D glasses only allow one of each of these images through to each eye. Your brain puts these images together and you're tricked into thinking that things are flying out of the screen – **POW!**

G

Glow for it

It's important to be seen, especially if you're out biking or walking in the dark. There are some cool materials that reflect light really well and seem to glow.

Toys or stickers that glow in the dark get "charged-up" by light and then let it out **v-e-r-y s-l-o-w-l-y**. The scientific name for this is **phosphorescence** (*say* fos-for-es-ense).

H

Healthy light

Sunlight is good for you. Our bodies need vitamin D to help get calcium from food. Calcium keeps our bones healthy. Our bodies get most vitamin D from being outside in the sunlight.

Incandescent light

Lots of heat means lots of light. Light made by heat is called **incandescent** (*say* in-can-des-ent) light. The most incandescent thing of all is the Sun – the source of almost all our light.

The electricity passing through the **filament** in this bulb makes it super-hot – then it burns really bright!

Heat in the filament lights up the bulb.

BUT (and this is important!) too much sunlight can burn your skin. If you are spending time in the sunshine, you will need to use sunscreen.

J

Joseph Swan

versus

Thomas Edison

K

Keep up the good work

SOLD OUT

The electric light bulb allowed people to work longer each day. Factories could work all night, and stores and restaurants stay open later. The light bulb was bad news for candlemakers though!

Englishman Joseph Swan invented the light bulb in 1879. But, so did American super-inventor Thomas Edison. *In the same year!* Both men had the same idea, but it is Edison we remember because he developed a bulb that was easier to make and sell.

Love LEDs

Light Emitting Diodes (LEDs) are little lights that make a big difference. They are small enough to fit into electrical circuits. LEDs use electronics and special materials to create light. They don't use heat like their big brother the **incandescent** light bulb and they use much less **energy**!

M

Mobile music

Today, music and other audio (books, radio programs, and podcasts) can be accessed on the Internet at any time. Look how far we've come at playing music on the move:

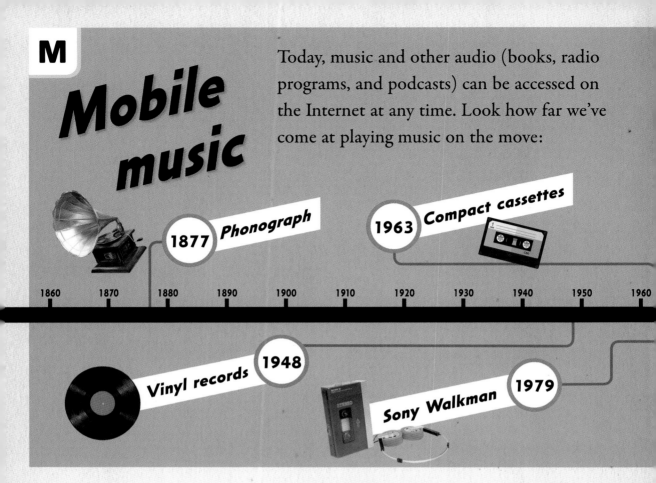

1877 Phonograph

1963 Compact cassettes

1860 | 1870 | 1880 | 1890 | 1900 | 1910 | 1920 | 1930 | 1940 | 1950 | 1960

Vinyl records **1948**

Sony Walkman **1979**

N

Night sky

Look up at the stars at night. How far away do you think they are? In space, stars and planets are a long way apart. Light from stars takes a long time to reach us on Earth.

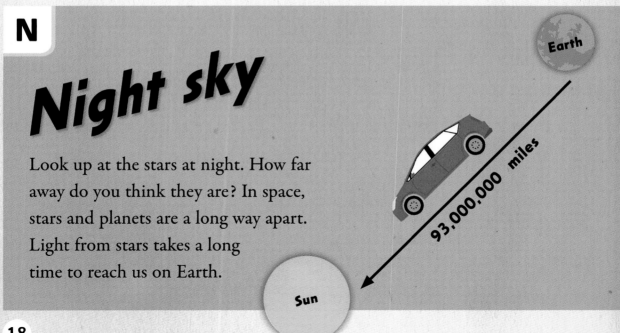

Earth

93,000,000 miles

Sun

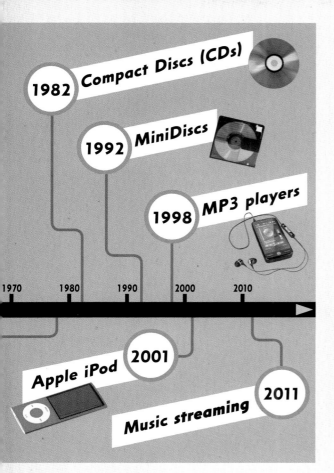

1982 Compact Discs (CDs)

1992 MiniDiscs

1998 MP3 players

1970   1980   1990   2000   2010

Apple iPod 2001

2011

Music streaming

O

Optical fibers

Light doesn't just ... light up. Light can also be used to transmit information. It is carried at **light speed** through fiber optic cables made of glass or plastic. Fiber optics zip cable TV and Internet into our homes.

The Sun is roughly 93 million miles away from Earth. Traveling at 60 miles per hour, it would take 177 years to drive that distance in a car! The Sun's light takes eight minutes to reach us.

Fiber optic cables carry information through light.

Phonograph first

Thomas Edison invented the phonograph in 1877. It was the first device that recorded and played back sounds. It used a moving needle (stylus) to turn vibrating sound waves into grooves in a tinfoil cylinder. Running the stylus back over the grooves would recreate the same **vibrations** and you'd hear the same sound played back.

Vinyl records used the same method as the phonograph.

Quiet, loud, weird, and scary

It can be difficult to record sounds for a film as the action happens, so some noises are added back in later. Adding sound effects such as footsteps or slamming doors to film or radio is called foley after Jack Foley, who began using them in 1927.

Try these foley sounds for yourself:

CRUNCHING SNOW

squeezing cornflour in a leather pouch

FLAPPING WINGS

flapping a pair of gloves

HORSES TROTTING

coconut shells tapped together

A foley artist recreates the sound of heavy rain.

21

R

Ready to record

Singers use microphones to record the sound of their voice. Inside the microphone is a disc called a diaphragm (*say* digh-a-fram) that collects the sound waves and vibrates. A magnet and coil of wire turn the **vibrations** into electrical signals which can be recorded.

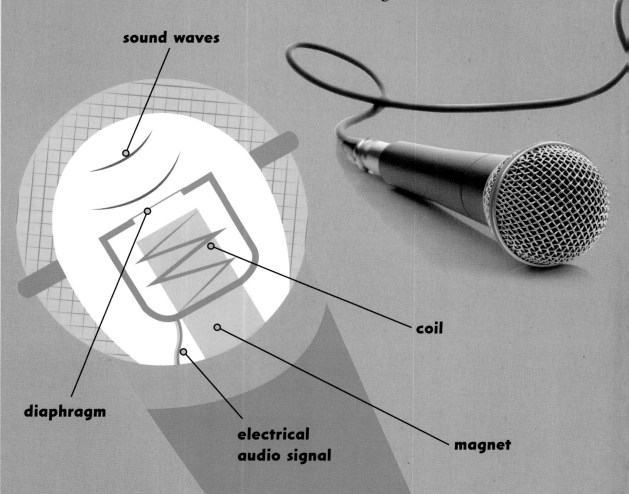

sound waves

coil

diaphragm

electrical
audio signal

magnet

Super speakers

Speakers work like microphones in reverse. Electrical signals are turned back into sounds by the magnet, coil, and speaker cone.

coil

electrical audio signal

magnet

speaker cone

You can **amplify** the sound of a speaker on a small music player by putting the speaker in a plastic cup or a bowl. Try it! Which homemade **amplifier** makes the best sound?

Traveling sound and light

T

Sound travels very quickly in all directions at once. In air it travels about 1,115 feet a second. That's fast!

Amazingly, some aircraft can fly faster than sound. When they do, they create a shockwave – a sudden **vibration** in the air – that makes a sound like thunder. This is called a sonic boom.

Ultrasound in echolocation

U

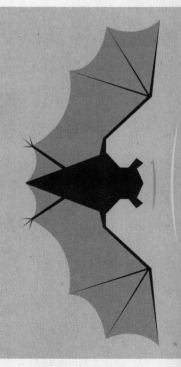

In a cave, the sound of your voice can come back as an echo. An echo is the sound waves bouncing off the walls back into your ears. Bats use echoes to find their way around and to hunt prey at night.

How long does it take from the time you flick on a switch for the light to come on? Try it! It seems to happen instantly, doesn't it? Well, it doesn't! But at a speed of about 984,000,000 feet a second. Light travels quicker than your eye can blink, so it seems instant.

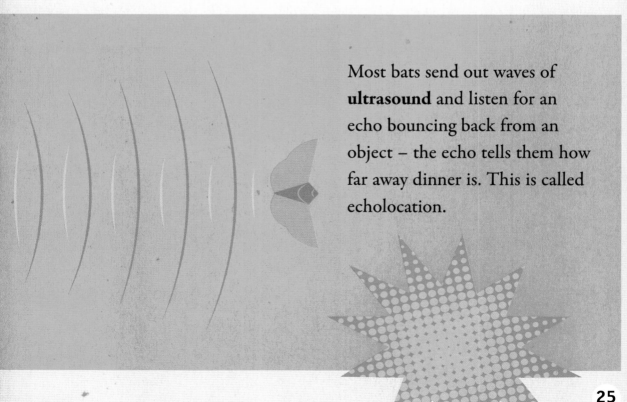

Most bats send out waves of **ultrasound** and listen for an echo bouncing back from an object – the echo tells them how far away dinner is. This is called echolocation.

Vibrations

The **BOOM** of a high-**amplitude** music concert or car stereo is largely the sound of the bass and drums. Loud, low-**frequency** sounds can make **vibrations** that we can feel *and* hear. They even vibrate the air in your lungs!

Weather clash

The sky goes dark, there's a flash in the sky and then – **BOOM!** In a thunderstorm, a clap of thunder is caused by a lightning strike. The lightning is incredibly hot and makes the air expand and vibrate very quickly. This makes the **BOOM** of thunder.

Lightning is the sudden release of a spark of electricity that builds up in storm clouds. It's really hot so it produces bright **incandescent** light.

We see lightning before we hear thunder because light travels faster than sound. Check it out next time there is a storm.

X

Xylophones

A xylophone is a **percussion** instrument made of wooden bars that you hit with a wooden mallet. Each bar is a different size and produces **vibrations** of a different **frequency** when you hit it. This is why each bar produces a different musical note.

Y

You can hear it!

Can you hear that? There is sound all around us. Most sounds travel as **vibrations** through the air, but those vibrations can travel through water and solid objects, too.

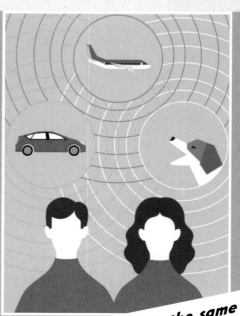

Sound travels in the same way, whatever is making it.

Zapped by lasers

In films, laser beams protect precious treasures from the bad guys, but they can be much more useful than that. A laser is an intense beam of light. With all that **energy** focused into such a narrow beam, they can cut things very precisely. Doctors use them in eye surgery or to weld body tissue together.

Lasers (less powerful than the eyeball-cutting ones!) are used at events to dazzle us and make the shows extra-cool and exciting.

Glossary

amplify: to make a sound louder

amplifier: a device to make sounds, such as music, louder

amplitude: how big a wave is – the distance of a wave from its starting point to its top or bottom

bioluminescence: a type of light created by chemical reactions that is given out by living things

energy: the ability to do work; making something work is the transfer of energy from one thing, or place, to another

filament: a thin wire inside a light bulb that produces light when heated by electricity passing through it

frequency: the number of waves made in a certain area over a certain time

human hearing range: the frequencies of sound that can be heard by humans

incandescent: a type of light produced by a hot, burning material

infrasound: sounds with frequencies below the frequency range that humans can hear

light speed: the speed at which light waves travel

percussion: musical instruments that you play by hitting or shaking

phosphorescence: a process where an object releases stored energy in the form of light over a period of time

streaming: a way that electronic data, like audio, is transmitted over the Internet

ultrasound: sounds with frequencies above the frequency range that humans can hear

vibration: a rapid movement back and forth of small things

wavelength: the distance between the high points of two waves

Index

About the Author

After learning about the history of everything at Goldsmiths College, I worked at the Science Museum in London, where I made record-breaking paper airplanes and set light to hydrogen-filled balloons. I have written and edited hundreds of books about subjects including BMX bikes, *Star Wars*, rescue vehicles, and dinosaurs. I live in Kent with my wife, daughter, and a cat with two names.

My love of very loud music, fireworks, and thunderstorms led me to write *Flashes and Bangs* and I hope you enjoy this book as much as I enjoyed writing it. Please shout about it if you do!